Inside to Outside

For Amy,
Who is a special poem.
and who writes special ones too!

Chris xo

CHRISTOPHER GUTKIND

Inside to Outside

Shearsman Books
Exeter

Published in the United Kingdom in 2006 by
Shearsman Books Ltd
58 Velwell Road
Exeter EX4 4LD

ISBN-10 0-907562-80-9

ISBN-13 978-0-907562-80-1

Acknowledgments and Thanks

I am grateful to the following publications in which the following poems first appeared although, perhaps, in a slightly different form: "Concentrate" in *Out of Our Heads*, "Shift" and "Notice" and "Swimming in America" in *Shearsman*, "To" in Staple, "tell me the rose" in *Odyssey*, "50 Hours in St. Marks" in *Oasis*, "Mould" and "Shift" and "Servings" in *The Stumbling Dance* (a Stride Publications anthology), part 1 of "Christian N" in *The Cancer Poetry Project Book* (though titled as "Snatching"), "Interactive" in the *San Francisco Bay Guardian* and "Another Day" and "Letter from an Asylum Home" in *Poetry Salzburg Review*.

I'd like to acknowledge Tony Frazer for believing in my poems enough to publish them – cheers Tony. And Hume Cronyn and Stephen Watts for helping me think about this collection.

I'd like to thank my family and friends and this good and difficult earth for supporting me, letting me grow, and celebrating me. I can't name people, there are too many of you and each has played a vital part, big or small, old or new, happy or painful. I love you all.

The publisher gratefully acknowledges financial assistance from
Arts Council England.

To Rilke
whose work always heals me
and helps me grow.

*... become the magic at the crossways of your senses,
be what their strange encounter means ...*

Sonnets to Orpheus
II:29
Translated by David Young

Contents

Inside to Outside

Opening

I gradually find myself
   reaching for you, those of you
still looking out.

So long as this world spins,
   knowing best
its own tone, this thin wafer of us

drawn in a circle – we jump
   to look,
itching to the beat

of such separate stories ...
   Voices we have heard but differently.
Variety might come

within a colour. But I can't
   stay inside too,
to help carry one corner: it teems

yet another breath beckons
   and maybe
we'll make some sense

in our chess, our chance ...
   I see someone's life is bent
into a question mark,

awake without an answer
   which
will gradually be felt –

my life taking its shape,
   the shape
taking its place.

I

(Figuring)

Mould

I am the still sometimes put hyphen
  between *non* and *fiction.*
   Or I tremble within it, haphazardly boring

a way out, falling off its end only to
  swing from a thread and crawl on its
   underside, easily, spinning back and forth

between its buttresses. (I'm that small.)
  If I stake all my dreams it's only
   not to lose my way, the view I've tended to

chip into, the sky stretching out loud
  when you're part of the furniture.
   Even after the sun ups and downs and after

the phones are put to sleep, the day's
  wounds are picked and licked and our
   ghosts tempted back in or out. No need to eat

but I'll weave a fudge to cast about.

Concentrate

What grim hardness it takes
  to get into shape, form a breath
    of fresh or stale air,
the old blood seeing new
    and slipping out.

Ink spills. My hand it cut.
  It can't hold a pen
    yet the drift is vital.
Why plug, stiffen, or agilitate
    this cycle of reach?

I would extend a foot
  past the edge of my mind's eye.
    It acts as a diving-board,
for a moment I'm unground
    and sinking.

The sense of this stays.
  It won't dissolve entirely
    but the taste might change
to become unpopular,
    as a guess is.

Shift

Privacy is a monastery –
  you didn't know, didn't want
    to know how much

I've cast and cut away,
  this life and that, pegged upon
    a different hand to strike

only here, paged in time
  and left in time, ghost of another
    couple of lovers who wake

to seek and find to explore,
  not what they don't know but
    what they do, now less

a mix, now again boring
  into a habit of mine, one I
    wear without you.

Angling

Who cares, give up, give in, breathe
   and begin again, anywhere,
  any thought, bounce from cost to cost,
    say *no*, say *yes*, say.

I care, come here, look on, feed
   upon my home, it moves,
  spins, picks loss from life and asks,
    needs a course, tops a course.

Why care, fall away, say away, watch
   not and know another knot,
  stay there, sound fair, soothe a sense,
    be a part, parting off.

Servings

My mind is lucid
senses tremble on a drop
a new music arrives
lifetimes shuffle off to sleep
fingers crook to write

I wait on each step.

Talking takes time
a fly buzzes by.
Maybe I'm amazed
figures guess during chess
words play in trust

voices jump.

Eyes change at night
a painting hangs still but trying
a swing swings empty
this piece is tiring
love comes and cries

I stop to cook.

Broken

I broke my heart,
    it wasn't working,
I've wandered off here, wandered off there,
    I was split so I split it more,
I broke my heart,
    I'm not asking.

I broke my heart,
    because it drifted off inside my head
which drifted farther off,
    I'm telling you this to help me,
I'm not asking it anything,
    the heart I broke.

I'm waiting, waiting,
    for its urges to collapse into me,
for it to house me again,
    my tired legs, my never-ending thoughts,
I'm telling you this my heart
    so faces stay beautiful.

My heart, my only,
    I'm just as sorry too,
wandering away to let yourself return
    is how broken I am,
speaking in restless dreams,
    calling me out.

Notice

I see ...

you must fill the gaps in,
  in the time being
before you,

this yawning space
  speckling with a few squares
to cope by and harbour in –

even they drift
  and shave the day away –
as life gives life unasked and needy

but lets you lay some holes
  along the way,
and you zip them up,

perhaps capturing a gift
  before being
replaced ...

inexactly.

II

(Homes)

Here

(I listen)

outside time
has changed back
and tonights will grow
after darkening
early

(a leaf gets weaker
with each wind
it rustles)

fall makes
poems drop from trees
who publish them that way
regardless of how
they're gathered

(fire is happiest
in unused
matches)

new hours
are called inside
and not knowing before
they explore
their home

(dust figures out
what air tries
to say)

Another Day

ducks do laps in the pond digressively
on new year's eve
but it's beyond that now

the revellers are already on their way home
wherever that is
and it is time to go to sleep

tomorrow we'll wake up and go for a walk
and wonder
what tomorrow brings

Life of a Name

Name
Visit
Home

Name

who did it belong to before
   or from its first utterance did it only own
sons and daughters?

was its first feature
   one of us, taking flight to another
to spread its essence?

its definition grew,
   spawning itself, each one speaking
something in common

and something else,
   its life becoming remote in age
till it called again

hearing a child answering
   what?

Visit

my name is mine
   yet it was given me by others
and others constantly use it

and I'm jealous
   of those flat worlds that wrap us up
to move about at leisure

where do they go,
   the ones that stay long enough
to decipher you?

have they slipped off
   their posts, bare and exposed
to make the day

for someone else?

Home

someone will be posted
   to what was mine, putting on
the watch I left off

what will they see,
   who will arrive to call it over
and over head home?

where is home?
   I think it's just a friend
that commutes

anywhere you know

[untitled]

tell me the rose
isn't obsessed
in what it does
its unfolding of space
its callings
as it draws a colour
up its stalk
to stroke our eyes
as our nose gets tugged
and softly kissed
or the day obsessed
by what it shows
the night by what it hides
the child in its play
its chasings
of dreams that open
and close
or us in our voices
saying anything
however veiled
however grey to be
pocketed
and fingered

Letter from an Asylum Home

early in this century
on a small piece of paper
she wrote
a letter to her husband

Sweetheart Come

in column after column
and line after line
in tight pencilled handwriting
she wrote

Sweetheart Come Sweetheart Come Sweetheart Come

she wrote
hundreds of the same words
over and over
and over each other

Sweetheart Come Sweetheart Come Sweetheart Come Sweetheart Come
Sweetheart Come Sweetheart Come Sweetheart Come Sweetheart Come

beside and into
and through each other
she repeated
this one intimate song

Sweetheart Come Sweetheart Come Sweetheart Come

in hope upon hope
and layer upon layer
in increasingly grey tones
she repeated

Sweetheart Come

she repeated it
until he became only a word
which could hardly
be seen

London

you home of ten years
and second birth of me

you world without centre
within the centre of my life

you wishing-well of faces
I draw upon to hear myself

you spring of busy streets
that finds me floating in ink

you hours of wandering laughter
I lock slowly into my belly

you unemployed afternoon
that makes me into an application

you library of parks and ponds
in the work my walks read

you shy families of fences
I too have felt and used

you busload of languages
for pressing my own in

you love of a lifetime
but no longer for me

III

(Circling Away)

Interactive

Whatever happened
to the kites
that just stayed up there?

You know the ones,
so difficult to launch,
taking ages to reach their limit

and even longer to reel in.
But mostly you just left them there
and waited, and watched.

And wondered.
About anything that came to mind.
It was a kind of exercise

for the spirit,
working on a line from ourselves
to what was almost immaterial –

a wavering dot,
without a care in the world
but staying up there –

almost out of time,
but holding on
at the same time.

It wasn't so long ago.
And maybe you wonder when it tilted
to the physical,

why it's all pull and jab,
quickness and control,
leverage and release.

You may have heard
it's about how time is spent.
Maybe you caught that.

Mother Time

It is my birthday.
I am thirty-three.
Thirty-three years ago

I was pushed and pulled
into this harder space
to begin my open-eyed growth here.

It is my birthday,
it is the anniversary of my entering,
of my opening out

into airy solidity,
far away from my liquid beginnings
and farther still

from the millisecond of hope
or – *(who can tell?)* –
absent-minded frenzy

that made me. Yes,
I am far into more measurable things now.
Look ... I look at my watch,

turn my wrist over,
perfectly – *(who can tell?)* –
as I've always done –

there's but fifty minutes left
to this space of a day,
this day of residue

that leans back and forth,
the sticky wake of an aging dream.
O what is time?

What is this thing we're in
that always goes past us
or stays still as we pass?

. . .

And how can I forget,
my dear mother,
how can I forget you?

You must have loved me enough
in whatever state I was in,
or before I even was,

since I still feel you inside
each dawning day, each hesitant dusk.
Mother, is it not

your birthday too,
the anniversary of the day
you cried to let loose

a beginning so far from your own?
O sad separation.
O endless addition.

Today you felt like the sun,
shimmering through me
in your ripe endurance

and unshadowed clarity,
whispering to the quiet ground
I was only walking on.

And your words became steps
making me
only as I took them.

. . .

Again the timeless uses us
in its changing and – *(who knows?)* –
perfect conversation,

coming and going even as we pass
each other – so often
unaware of other steps inside

or beside us. I watch ...
it doesn't always pass by.
Sometimes it's us passing life by.

Sometimes we just walk away or recoil,
anxious for another state,
far from probability.

And sometimes we grow with it,
from fate, to fate,
in as many ways as we are,

along the umbilical allowance of our lives.
And what am I doing
but about to begin another new day,

about to leave the day
I've come to adore,
which has happened forever now,

will never be nothing now,
unlike tomorrow,
you once unbroken promise,

old unborn tomorrow,
always waiting,
always splitting and disappearing,

into the next tomorrow,
into a new today,
yet another today,

you about to contain me again,
you once enough,
you once endless thing

where all my needs
fulfilled and renewed themselves
in your unmeasured,

now crowded space.
And if these days
we meet less for being too full,

you're still on course,
still recognizable in the skin
that covers me too,

still a kind of unavoidable growth
I can't really gather
but can't help be as well.

Even my yesterdays
follow you along,
needing you to need me now and again,

remembrance like a battery,
different energies
making or breaking,

each of us a little spark of proof,
wanting to be caught
before we go,

wanting to be asked for.
I suddenly find myself listening out
for my name

but it's so silent it feels
like I must have
just called someone.

. . .

And I'm waiting.
I suddenly find myself burning
in this space awhile.

How long will I burn
I wonder?
Then all these things start

suggesting again,
start their continuing again,
the wondering both burn and balm,

always caught between,
making by settling.
Maybe I'm in the middle of something,

some endless opening
I never asked to attend.
But each day I ask it more.

I don't know what it is mother.
Yet every day or so
whatever it is finds me,

seems to have passed through you
on the way to me,
on the way to another,

calling to calling.
We don't even have to be
near each other.

. . .

Tonight it was the moon
and you were waiting for anything
to lightly lay upon,

to rest your open eye upon,
sharing or – *(who can tell?)* – shedding
what you saw on the other side.

I just happened to look up
and catch you.
You felt me turning,

before I knew you surrounded me,
before I knew you,
before you knew me.

And then, just now, it's late at night.
Unable to resist
we've crossed into another day,

another watch we wind in and out of,
another fleshy daydream
my fingers have to measure by.

They listen to it saying,
they listen to what it doesn't say
and what it can't say.

Then my eyes listen too,
gathering, like yours, and speaking.
(Inbetween I take a step.)

(Inbetween I take a guess.)
I'm not trying to do anything
but I can't help doing it.

I was thinking ... it's a way
of seeing ...
stroking something

that never stops.

Supermarket

I go into the supermarket,
seem to leave myself outside.

Above me the PA system gives out soft music
or deals they want me,
me as well, to know about.

Around me are other people,
vaguely or really there, shopping.
Around me are the products we call home.

I step into the aisle of boxes they call cereals.
I stand before them,
wavering, feeling dizzy, uneasy.
So many: a hundred, maybe a hundred and fifty varieties.

I can't find the one I want.
Too bad they don't have more,
one more, mine.

I walk out. I seem to rejoin myself.
People wander, cars go by,
in the greater market they call community.

They have made it look so real,
so like it's supposed to be like this.

Triptych

(Click-Click)

I remember
I think
a time of less data

when you could feel something
before you looked

a moment less screened
while you looked

when you could
feel something

a time of more time
(as if outside time)
if and when and after you looked

I think
I remember

I think

I'm a flower becoming data.
(There's music but it doesn't matter.)

A glassy page revs in around me –
                    where are you, where am I?
(It matters but it doesn't matter.)

There's music but it doesn't matter.
(Who knows, who knows what your smile
                        is made of.)
Is that the screen moving or me?
Is that a screen or a street before me?

Where are you, where am I?
(I'm waiting for a friend but it doesn't matter.)

There's a little link: it's someone.
            Click-Click: smile a word or word a smile.
(It's nothing but it doesn't matter.)

Never mind who that *you* is: it's someone too.
(It's enough but it doesn't matter.)

There's matter but it doesn't music.
(I'm a window that can't see –
                who is out, who is in, who is?)
Is that me or the screen moving?
Is that me or the screen smiling?
Is that me or is that me or is that me or is that me or is that ...

Who is out and who is in?
        A glassy page revs away from me.
(It's real but it doesn't matter.)

There's music but it doesn't matter.
(I'm a flower becoming data.)

I think
I see

a time when you won't see
without screening

when the flesh has been machined
and every thought too

and every thought data
somewhere far away

(inside you but away)

so they seem sent to agree
to a schedule
you seem to agree to

which everyone gathers
(and gathers for)
when everyone gathers without meeting

when someone is a projection
you see

or something
you think

Montague Road ...

The singing tree of Leytonstone sings
   almost everyday,
  without a hiccup,

without a doubt in its calling.
   But the first time I passed it it seemed
  to hesitate,

make me one of its internal messages,
   sing me in and then
  sing me out again.

So now, perhaps, it doesn't notice me,
   nor do I notice it as much.
  We've each become part

of the street, the houses,
   the air of the place, the birds
  you hardly ever see.

       . . .

But over the houses and past
   the tower blocks, on the flat fields
  where players play

and goalposts are laid like a croquet set
   for giants, where I was
  walking one afternoon,

there the ground is speckled
   with black dots, crows, pecking
  amongst the grass,

rising up and coming down again,
   puppets without strings.
  And I was a newcomer,

wandering between their lines,
   tripping over the myth
  of their constancy.

Eclipsed

We couldn't do anything about it.
It just happens.
(We can only watch,
measure, wonder, wait.)

I walked outside, left work, following ...
Others were there, we knew it was going to happen.
(The sky got darker, we felt something wide,
perhaps we felt water.)

People looked up, looked at each other,
talked, laughed nervously.
(Then our skins were just enough
to stop us spilling.)

We tilted our thinness
back into the daytime air.
(We thought of ourselves only
filling and unfilling.)

IV

(Elsewhere)

Around Us

the universe
is a minute
and almost weightless inkling,
among many,
in the corner of someone's daydream,
someone who lives
way outside of us,
though we live in them,
and who is about to
make us centre-stage in a fleeting musing,
a fleeting musing
that feels like it's always been there
and which actually is
billions of our years,
but even now as this someone
starts to see more
and more clearly
the worlds and space and time
we're part of,
right down to our faces,
a friend is about
to disturb him,
because they're late,
their break is over,
and others
are waiting

50 Hours in St. Marks

the park was full
today
then I'm here

   . . .

bodies lie (aboutness)
and wards
whiz by

yes
I am going to cut up
my time

   . . .

cures all along
begin
by examination

numbness
to poetry
before anything happens

quiet night
spotted
with feet

   . . .

growing light
a plumbing operation beside me
succeeds

(woken-up
by gurgles so I filled
them in)

couldn't sleep
but eyes close
without wanting

. . .

soon to go in
about
to be hyphened

kept white
because pink is too close
to truth

needle

butt ouch
and maybe
it's working

slow to find nothing
a gain
I suppose

now I feel
much less
than I should

buzzed and stopping
want
to walk

. . .

bad floral patterns
can be good
for one hour

cleaners talk domestic
over the wall
and something is received

   . . .

taken to those
who
open you

(going off
without caring
to bye)

operating
though
I don't know

   . . .

awoke (no dreams)
to find
all blur

(a most lovely
oxygen
comes to help me)

hallway parents
see me
strange

yes they are angels
of a sort
always checking

   . . .

nice pills
asshole ring muscle cut hurts
if moving

sleep again
till 1 a.m. frenzy nearby
and nothing

(I'm aware
of a deep scary
in groggy)

. . .

gentle ward
full of pains
and endings

Christian N

1

snatches of speech one flight up   the old
are playing with gadgets   cancer toys
with pumps and buttons   insertions instructions
that the young devised

it's all so serious now   it's all to the end
to the prize   life   detaching without any time for us
looking back   in surprise at our surprise

how could it be over how could it be   the
final over   nothing left but leftovers
people places things   playthings we took   up
still talking   gossiping good

2

and all the efforts of death
are there

the pills
the plants
the ready-made meals

the tapes
replacing books

the friends
family
the naps

the caring
too much
the every move

and the focus
of everything
the unceasing
outside

the quick loss
of balance
the touchiness

the embarrassment
you feel

the something
new to you

the facing
unfacing

the everyday last
and lasting

the through

3

another
  of their number gone,
a life of their lifetime here,

and she will never know this gathering
  where they talk
their versions of her together

though she may have
  imagined it beforehand,
all the pieces belonging so-so

as they slowly head home,
  not wanting it to end, this concoction
of carriers of a part of you,

the traces tender,
  the touch impossible to resist,
so yielding

she can carry us
  through
the day

dividing night

Bosnia (the Field) on the Radio

everyone there
died that day   some more
             than others

it was
the last thing in their lives
that happened

men sent
explosions   some exploded people
             into pieces

a man looking
saw a boy's brains spill
out of his eyes

sudden helpers
tried keeping someone's broken head together
with their hands

cars carts and arms
were used   screaming and rushing
             used too

insufficient backup
meant insufficient help
was arriving

various
interpreted massacres formed
within hours

outside
of the war zone   voices
lives   were calmer

To

the hair to touch
the shoes to walk
the glasses to see
the luggage to go seek

the curls to fondle
the laces to learn how to
the eyes to find another
the travel to Auschwitz

the strands to be cut
the feet to be walkless
the staring to be still
the exploration to cease

V

(Things)

Apple

Apple, what do you know?
  How is it you became such a myth
that someone had to bite you
  and another record you?

(In your roundness we find wisdom,
  in your uneven roundness experience
and still greater wisdom.)

Aren't you one of the earth's many spies,
  attracting us to see what we're about inside?

(In your skin we sense humility
  and courage: unafraid of breaking
your only fear is of being partially eaten,
  kept in separate places.)

But you're about as blind as we are,
  the time of any true correspondence
is long since over: as you fill us
  we can only fill you with basic imaginings.

(In your flesh we taste strength,
  in your core the seeds of another,
your concerns and hope for the future.)

Apple, what do you know now?
  Aren't you becoming increasingly virtual,
full of being projected, like us,
  getting to know things second-hand?

(In your stem we feel our separation:
  we will never know what you know.)

Apple, you once apple, it seems
  we'll pass on the way to rootlessness.
Eve wouldn't touch you now.

Commuter Man

Commuter man, what are you
  thinking about, standing there, waiting?
Could it be you're empty-headed
  from the last round of scurrying?

Who knows what's going on in you.
  Maybe it's last night or, like me,
maybe it's the poster you're unbusy reading.

Everything's changed but everything's the same:
  week after week I'm part of this dim parade,
these silent musical chairs, the shuffling
  as one of us disappears.

You too. And year after year. You see me. I see you.
  At most we notice if the other's got new shoes
or a different magazine telling us what to do.

We come and go in this tradition: rushing
  outside, queuing up, milling about, being crushed
into someone's eyes, a little glance,
  perhaps, carried by the crowd.

So close, so far: I'll never know, I haven't a clue.
  You are, indeed, just a man, only you,
only, for a moment, me and you.

Everything's so routine it's almost holy:
  we ride up the escalators and open the doors
of our mostly mortgaged lives,
  hoping for a little air on the way.

O commuter man, undistract yourself
  from your newspaper, if once, and tell me,
how is it you're so able to switch on,
  and then, switch off?

Or is this just the effect
  of another dance, another distance
we're on the way to?

Table

Table, why so still?
  Is it to show us we can move,
settle down, take off again?

Empty you're an advert for loneliness,
  you only really belong
when something's on you: bowl of soup, cup of tea,
  arms, letters, dreams.

(Something of your surface is always with us,
  the earth's an endless table
our feet know, or don't, over and over.)

At home, in too many homes, you're the heart
  I've always milled around,
I've watched you in your waiting only to wonder who,
  or what, I was watching.

(Or words, maybe they're your lightest
  and heaviest inhabitant,
flying back and forth, and then, hesitating.)

Sometimes, sitting down to you,
  my legs brush against yours, conjuring up others,
softer, warmer, weaker ones
  who turned and walked away.

We can't stop sitting down to ourselves
  with you.
We can't stop remembering.

Body

Body, what do you long for?
  Is it true your sense of separation
will never go away?

Inside you're mostly water,
  your liquid roots are still working,
but that doesn't make you sail over to someone
  or let someone seep into you.

How you long to be a bigger ocean again,
  to leave hands and feet behind, walls, roads, dreams.

You'd like to unzip your skin,
  feel your bony shores dry themselves out
and watch your exotic organs swim free.

But you can't, can you?
  There's no way out, time's erased the zipper,
it's only you, and I, trapped together,
  unable to be without the other.

Still, sometimes I see another close by
  and I think you sense them too,
feel the pull, the tide, swell against your skin.

It's them you feel separate from now isn't it,
  another body, another history, yet another possibility?

Almost everyday we're inches,
  seconds away, but almost everyday we turn.
You play your part: touch isn't touch,
  you seem to say, without space.

Body, body me, will you be happier
  when you're made more metally,
when you've lost the loss of larger, older currents?

Perhaps you'll be part of some
    orchestrated, digitized family, attached
but unaware you still walk alone.

And perhaps I won't even be able
    to remind you.

Morning

Morning, what are you made of?
   How is it that, such a weightless carrier,
you always carry everything?

You must be one of time's untiring gatherings,
   pushed and pulled in unison:
as you run out here you're off on another beginning.

(I climb out of bed and into your expanding envelope –
   but I'm just a bit of dust in your wind.)

Somedays you're a child full of promise,
   your breakfast is a dream,
but other days you wake up distant and dreary,
   too many yesterdays have passed.

(I look into the mirror and splash some water on my face –
   it's my way of making sure I'm together again.)

You allow everything to pass and return
   in endless variation,
you have no choice: our difference is we're stuck
   in something that ends.

(I eat, check my mail, listen to the news, make a call –
   I'm already too busy to notice you leave.)

Still, as you temporarily disappear,
   only to reappear elsewhere, turning over
whatever you've weathered,
   do you miss some previous cargo?

Or in that daily swipe of your memory
   can anything really matter?

VI

Allakariallak and Flaherty of the North

This is a record,
   it captures sound,
and when you play it you hear
   what you've captured,
and the sound remains the same,
   each time.

But we've gone too far,
   let's start at the beginning,
or what we reckon – *(it's about 1921*
   in this reckoning) – to be the beginning,
or what we decide to remember
   as the beginning ...

It's the "trader" presenting the gramophone.
   No – the students come to see a film,
they gather (gradually), sit down (often talkatively),
   the lights dim (preparatorily)
and it is silent,
   that is how it started,

how it must have begun, this time,
   or continued – *(yes, that's better)* – this time.
But the "trader" presents too –
   (what does he want?) –
and it's brown on white, hard against soft,
   all square-edged and noticeable

before the white wall of billowing furs.
   "Nanook" is curious ...
someone has caught this – *(silently?)* –
   someone has gone up there for this – *(it is already 1921)* –
been backed for this, casted and pointed
   a camera for this ...

and he touches its difference – *there* –
   its outsideness. (And the other – *framing* –
the one you don't see.)
   (And it's the first time – *even if it isn't* –
just like that.)
   And it's all out in front of you (us),

it's in your (our) eyes,
   the "trader" puts a record on,
puts what's inside for him on – *(how far has it travelled?)* –
   winds its mechanical heart up,
puts the needle over,
   then down

and starts it,
   its *continuation* starting again,
the frozen sound – whatever it is sounding impossible
   to "Nanook" – some split-second
without cause – *(it's that scary)* – but the spirit
   rebelling, seeking –

some "knock-knock" captured so far away,
   coming to life ... starting, filling, dispersing ...
entering him – *(does it?)* –
   letting him in – *(does it, really, and*
does he go in?).
   (Remember, it's the first time.)

Then ...
   an almost imperceptible start.
No – "Nanook" listens and then starts.
   (Remember, this is a record, let's be accurate,
mark it down.)
   He looks closer,

he touches the box that the sound
    comes from –
(would you do that? – it's too late isn't it –
    you've seen the record) –
he does that studying thing,
    the investigation

within investigation,
    following the action back –
(but you've seen that – good) – and quickly,
    looks on each side of the box,
quick and hard,
    and quick again,

closer now and –
    but no, there's no movement,
no give, nothing to be seen.
    And now he looks at us,
smiles, laughs, the eyes shiny like a thousand stars –
    are they crying? –

a thousand tales or a thousand tellers
    of one tale,
a thousand versions ...
    looking out at us, full of an insideness
we don't know
    but maybe we can *(yes –*

you are good) capture it,
    looking and ...
you, out there, over here, attending
    or tending, exploring or ...
what do we do here, do we touch it, set in its setting? –
    here and there – shimmering out

75

into a camera or the man behind it
   or, besides him, might there be a relative
out watching, out listening in? –
   (makes sense doesn't it, that smile,
the eyes like a …).
   No, he doesn't know it's us, not yet –

(what will he think?*)(no, please, leave that) –
   doesn't really know – *(or does he?)* –
that he's being frozen,
   that he's *becoming* … what we're good at,
silently … what we will know,
   second by second, progressively,

what he won't know,
   this time, a record to pan over,
enriching us – *(even if it's …)* –
   but he doesn't know he's enriching us,
by his own exertion,
   his own wage,

or does he? *(Try that.)*
   But what's this,
so bored so soon? – *(yes, let's look at him too)* –
   the "trader" removes the record,
tries to – seems to – *(that soft shore always allowing)* –
   seems to –

tries to explain where the sound
   comes from.
No, it's not in the box –
   "Nanook" had pointed to the gramophone –
it's in the round thing – *and now the "trader"*
   in his pointing –

it's in here, in here!, in here!,
 words – *(what are they anyway?)(careful!)* –
and pointing,
 words, if he had any,
failing him.
 (There is no way to describe this.)

Finally, we cut, move to another
 scene, and another – the recording always
hungry, hunting, planning – and "Nanook" is caught doing
 something else, something with a considered
agility about it –
 (what should we do after the film?) –

scuttling across the white ice floes,
 which white we don't know,
we hadn't yet noted their 13 words for it –
 (I heard that somewhere) –
hadn't yet recorded them, froze
 them, packed them,

unpacked them, thawed them,
 played them ...
unafraid when our own language
 is back there – *inside and outside* – waiting.
(But it's the end of all that,
 said again, said again, said again,

so take it off, it keeps skipping.)
 But but – it continues – this is an edit –
this is a record –
 it captures sound – *(was it really quiet?)* –
and (almost) every tale you tell will come across
 the same,

and (almost) every tale
   you tell will come out the same,
and almost every tale you tell,
   and almost every tale,
and almost,
   and.

* He won't. Allakariallak died of
starvation 2 years after filming.

VII

(Elegies)

Airport Fish (SFO)

You look like toys to us now,
swimming back and forth
in your watery, glass cages,
but the most perfect toys –
lifelike, animal, fluid.

(Our eyes have changed.
The hunter invents the prey.)

Where are you travelling to
you little far-flung fish?
I see you scaling great heights
only to forget how to swim,
only to stop and stare.

Swimming in America

America is a weapon of mass destruction.
(Overheard 2/98)

1

I step in and hold my breath.
Sometimes it seems that everything is
swimming here, almost drowning,
every person who has ever lived only allowed
to play out themselves,

until they're consumed, raining
in one hard song, and then
straight into the ground.
Full of sound it is, full of moving voices.
I use my ears to breathe.

I use my ears to stop and think.
Faces begin to speak.
They look like buried tears, the eyes sound worried,
you can hear them reassure themselves:
I'm okay, you're okay, I'm ...

2

O broken record, CD, website or
whatever of the ebbing breath,
what forecasts are you pumping out now?
Are not poets still overflowing
in magical supermarkets?

The echoes keep me on edge.
A damp discord begins.
You can almost hear the laughing of hyena cries,
the squall of residual say-so,
preying from the inside out as they pray.

I wander the aisles for my needs,
for products to call home.
We wait in line for our plastic communion,
the ringing-up of authorizations,
another dawn, another shower.

3

Mostly the world's worn
as an import here.
You can gather excited talk about the latest
older culture as dress,
or our own amphibious varieties,

synthesized down to a sentence.
We are good with words, good with their edges.
I swim tepidly, half in fear.
The ground has soaked up too much water.
Our constructions float.

Even the ghosts of yesterdays and others
have risen against our ears.
One, two, three, four,
we don't want a racist war!
Soon, fish will walk here.

4

Wait, the wettest winter
is almost over. And the olympics of ships
and missiles has spit itself out.
It floats and waits too,
for far-flung franchises to open

and flowers to turn into data ...
Dear earth, dear erotic earth
you were once called, and called to
inside the voice of our lungs.
You would answer back

with a breeze or stillness.
Or with countless other leaderless graces
that rowed inside us.
I can't think without your patter.
But I'll learn, like genes discovered.

5

News item: *KFC and BK doing well*
in Pakistan. Hundreds more to be built.
And if you put your ear
to the sea-shells on the shores there,
you can hear the cogs flutter.

(Sometimes it seems the whole world
is swimming in America.)
It sounds like it was meant to be something else.
But now the future's a drink
in the glass of your eye,

the air between us unbreedable.
And as I melt away
into the meals of techno-mystics,
I let my hand sponge a breath from the palm
of something drifting by me.

6

Almost out of voice
I'm switched on to water and it works ...
Even if some of us don't have
our fins, are inbetween,
unable to stir, unable to sleep.

Then there's the problem
of horizons being tossed into nets, but escaping,
or baby implants talking
before being born, and drowning.
There is much to do.

Somewhere, someone hasn't learned.
I have the odd dream
about dripping into one.
And I hear them tell pollinating stories
that remind me of air.

Dying Sunflower

You tall tortured king,
following the light
you feel, the smile you crave,

the look you can't bear
to look away from.

Now you've bowed your head again,
and for the last time,
though it's not even dusk.

Now even your wing-like leaves
roll and twist inwards.

Soon they'll crack and break,
your scrawny torso
will shiver and fall into its plush entourage,

which only looks up at you now,
waiting, a bit fearful,

while beside you still stands half an old stem,
your mother perhaps,
a crutch you'll never use.

And not even your dangling children
can help you now,

they're just a hungry necklace,
a fleshy weight
out to take your colour,

like the crown of sun-flash
now split among them.

But still we look into your lovely
dark night, drinking
our softest, saddest selves.

And you, you have finally,
suddenly noticed us.

You look perplexed
and a bit sad too.
Everything happened so soon.

the Planes, the Buildings, the World

The plane went into the building
but it did not come out.
Then another plane went into the next building
but it did not come out either.

It was as though plane and building were made
for each other, like they had waited
their whole lives for this and could finally
die now, feeling completed.

While down on the streets and around the world
most of us only kept watching,
half-expecting the planes to come out again,
but they didn't, they just disappeared.

And then the buildings disappeared too,
just dropping into the ground
like summer sandcastles, taking what they knew
with them, their lives and their loves,

their yesterday, their today, and tomorrow,
their jacks and jokers, kings and queens,
their plans and orders, their secrets and dreams,
their faraway views and executions.

Inbetween

Men and women come and go ...

Out while they're walking,
and talking in the time they have to talk,
they still look around,
listening for the sound of what-to-do.

You can see them working or playing
like there's nothing inbetween ...

They carry bags, still, and maps,
and now phones, and other pieces of our soft heroics.
They carry their home in a voice or two.

Men and women come and go ...

I'm asked directions as we pass.
It leads to a little lifetime between us,
a little taking-place,
before I take my things and go.

VIII

2000-2170

2000

It's not that
something ended
and something started.

Switching on: a wishful current
transfers from the flesh.

But that when we looked
we could see
another beginning.

Click-click: a pulsing of usefulness
felt in the wiry brain.

The pausing to remember
whatever once
happened to us.

Suspend: a rest for the system
of metal make-believe.

That everyone was as you,
a thinker, a dreamer,
a flyer, a survivor.

2020

I flew into the inside,
　a metallic wind
at my back, before me
　the cover of lives to choose from,
the latest surge of being
　of our selves.

I flew into it
　because it carried me,
into its quick hive of hopeful convenience,
　screened through,
each of us passing without
　touch or sting.

I flew and I flew desperately,
　trying to get away
but hang on, the flesh always feeling
　more lost, taken up,
implanted, powered on,
　on the outside.

2050

I ... I'm trying
to think ... to say ...

Program: *Welcome, lie back and relax,*
wait for the cue,
pick your program.

too little time ... to say
everything ... I ...

Program: *Your mind is shared,*
your body far away,
prepare for insertion.

I ... oh think! ...
we ... wanting more ...

Program: *Your processing has begun,*
from your own desire,
to the end of your skin.

leaving ... now ...
new ... I ...

Program: *Soon you will wake,*
happy in your home,
in your gods and heroes.

I ... oh ...
hello.

2080

Thanks be to you
   little gods, soft sapiens –
thank you for being,
   for being yourselves enough to disappear,
thank you, to you
   we owe everything.

We figured it out,
   we have, we have, we have ...

And to you great ones,
   matter and chance,
everything that is and can be, everything time allows –
   thank you forever and ever again,
for you are the possibility
   of our becoming.

We look forward,
   we do, we do, we do ...

We thank each of you
   for your breath,
your strong tools, your supple dreams –
   and we give these thanks,
take these thanks,
   and swallow them.

2120

In pockets
and hard to reach places
some of us survive.

They think:
Our place was everything,
the sense of our doing
and everything else.

Not in charge anymore,
unable to do what the others do,
they can't come close,
remaining fiercely themselves,
fresh and human.

And they say:
We live between natures and certainties,
chemistries and physics,
we guess to know.

Refusing to fuse themselves,
happy not to be new,
looking at their heavens
and their hells, their suffering
is almost over.

They feel:
Only what's inside is real,
the rest is far away
and past us.

Far from now
and dying we'll hope
for miracles.

2150

It's stiff in here
  but it's always working.

We harvest the laws
  of nature, exactly and deeply,
with no space for subtlety
  or relaxation.

We gather there
  because that is where we exist,
wired into the long sun
  to take our fill.

We tick away
  to the end, coiled and captured
in another's hard field
  and season.

It's our own
  agricultural revolution.

2170

A photo was found
many years from now.

One machine said:
we look so different from them.

Various people looking out,
unreal in their fragility.

Another machine said:
it's hard to believe we were that.

Wondering out of ourselves,
awaiting our new body.

Finally they thought:
we're very lucky to be here.

And flying out of time
and out of space.

Notes

Angling. To Samuel Beckett whose explorations have informed this piece, specifically his *Texts for Nothing.*

Letter from an Asylum Home. Dedicated to and based on a letter by Emma Hauck (1878-1928), written in 1909, in which the words *Herzensschatzi Komm* were written over and over. It was part of an exhibit called *Art and Psychosis* at the Hayward Gallery in London in 1996-97.

Mother Time. To my mother.

Christian N. Landlady and friend of four years. It should be said that the end of part 3 comes from listening to *Break on Through* by The Doors.

To. Based on a visit to the museum at the former Nazi concentration/ extermination camp of Auschwitz, in Oswiecim, Poland.

Allakariallak and Flaherty of the North. This piece is based around an early "ethnographic" film, *Nanook of the North*, made by Robert Flaherty in Northern Canada in 1921, and the screening of this film to an ethnographic film class. As well, additional information, which entered or informed this poem, was found in the 1988 book by Richard Barsam, *The Vision of Robert Flaherty: the artist as myth and filmmaker.* I wish to acknowledge Jorie Graham, elements of whose writing style I have consciously borrowed, and Adrienne Rich's book of essays, *What is Found There*, as influences behind this poem.

Airport Fish (SFO). SFO is the aviation symbol for San Francisco airport. This poem stems from the aquaria in the domestic terminal.

Swimming in America. The italicized bits in parts 3 and 5 are taken from news items on the radio. The one in part 4 is from a poem, *Moors Above Walsden*, by Stephen Watts.

Dying Sunflower. After Schiele's *Sunflower II.*

Inbetween. It should be said that the repeated line here is a variation of Eliot's in his *Prufrock.*

2120. Part of the 6th stanza closely echoes Rilke in part 3 of his sequence, *The Island*, where he writes 'Only what's inside is near, the rest is far away' (translated by Franz Wright). (*Die Insel*. 'Nah ist nur Innres; alles andre fern'.)

Christopher Gutkind

I was born in 1963 in The Hague to an American mother and British father, the latter British by virtue of being a German-Jewish refugee in the UK from 1939 and throughout the war. We soon moved to Montreal where I spent most of my first twenty-four years, except for a year in Nigeria at 7 and a year in Edinburgh at 13. My father was an urban anthropologist and my mother a librarian. I grew up with three older sisters. My parents were politically left but in many ways I had a conventional North American middle-class upbringing and experience. Sports and crap tv played an enormous part in my life there. Somehow that changed. At McGill University I studied History and Literature and then I moved to London in 1988. I studied Librarianship at the University of London and then lived here for 10 years and it is here that I started writing poetry seriously. Hence most of my work has been published in the UK although that is a very small amount. I lived in Berkeley, California, from 1999-2003 and I have British, American, and Canadian citizenship, something which has given me a very strange sense of home. I consider myself Atlantic in basis but International in outlook. I've done plenty of odd jobs but since 1989 I've worked in libraries, currently at the School of Oriental and African Studies, London. I doubt I'll ever leave this island. My religion is wonder, astonishment, possibility.

Comments or queries are welcome at cgutkind@yahoo.com or via www.myspace.com/outernet if I'm still there.

Lightning Source UK Ltd.
Milton Keynes UK

176648UK00001B/49/A

9 780907 562801